From School of Business to Corporate America

"How to Knock Down the Barriers"

Isiah Reese

From School of Business to Corporate America

Copyright © 2007 by Isiah Reese

ISBN 978-1-4357-0163-2

Acknowledgments

I would like to thank my family and true friends for all of their support. My journey to become a highly educated individual was driven by my faith in God and his son Jesus Christ. I have been blessed to learn from some of the greatest minds in the world today. My corporate career took a young man from a small rural town in South Carolina to the other side of the world and back. I draw my inspiration from those that I keep close in my life.

I was taught to believe in my core values and to never forget that the people you pass going up are the same you would pass going down when you forget where you came from. I am proud to say, that I never forget Murphy Street in Sumter, South Carolina and running barefoot on it before it got paved.

"Success comes to those that take it, not those that wait for it."

Isiah Reese- Author

Foreword

"Isiah is equipping the next generation of students with key tips that it took me years to learn on my journey through West Point and an MBA from Stanford. The difference is that it will cost them far less money and pain."

    Noah Johnson MBA, Corporate Strategy and
    Insight Wal-Mart Stores, Inc.

"Outstanding! A must read for every college student and should be included with every freshman orientation class. Simple, real world techniques to maximize your college experience."

    Lionel Riley, President Future Solutions Now

"The future success of our world is built on the backs of an educated society. It is our responsibility to uplift those around us and not be fearful of retribution. Isiah Reese has taken critical steps to bring a level of understanding to tomorrow's leaders, pressing them to go above and beyond their comfort zone and challenge the status quo while remaining true to themselves. 'If we want future generations to get to where we are then we are responsible for blazing a trail, outstretching our hands and leaving a legacy. If you do all of this effectively, then breadcrumbs on the path are unnecessary!'"

    Timothy Howell, MBA Director of Diversity
Corporate Manager

Introduction

The Business School Student's Guide to Corporate America

I vividly remember some friends questioning my decision to attend a Historically Black College Universities (HBCU) to further my studies. There were some harsh comments made and quite honestly, they were ill informed statements being made by 18 year old kids. Here they were making a decision about the rest of my life. I would say to myself, "Hmm... and you were my counselor in high school when?" I guess they felt a sense of what I called later in life, a "Superiority Complex of thyself".

I have not held that against them. They were accepted into some of the finest institutions in the country. Somehow they felt that my accredited University was not up to par. It is a landmark institution and most of their parents attended that same University. These conversations actually fueled my natural competitive innate nature to achieve more and resulted in me entering my HBCU with a sense of attitude. I also realized that my friends were fast becoming a word that would be common in my vocabulary in corporate America; they were _Associates_ not _"Friends."_

My decision to attend an HBCU was like going from good to great. The social life was much better! It's funny how my *associates* would attend my homecoming events, yet they didn't view my University as being up to par. The opportunity to meet a compatible person was much greater due to the fact that there were and are more black women attending HBCU's than men. I felt a sense of FAMILY when attending my HBCU. Walking into the dining hall and smelling food like "Mama" used to cook reminded me of home. During my stint at the university I built strong friendships. Some of these friendships have lasted longer than the relationships I built with the people I grew up with. Pledging a Greek fraternity or sorority was an option if that was your chosen way of life. This too, gave me a sense of family. I know "Stomp the Yard" gave viewers a glimpse of Greek life, but being "on the YARD" at an HBCU was a reality. I took the opportunity to experience all aspects of becoming a more mature young black man during my tenure at my HBCU. I played football, enjoyed having a social life, pledged Omega Psi Phi Fraternity Inc, and got what I believe is the most important thing of all, a fully accredited degree from a great business school.

From my experiences at my HBCU I gained a sense of self and a clear vision of who I would become. I listened intently as my professors hammered the point that you had to be TWICE AS GOOD, WORK TWICE AS HARD, AND THAT STILL WOULD NOT BE ENOUGH to measure up or compete in corporate America! I think they enjoyed the notion that they were forming great minds. They had to let us know that we were not inferior individuals because we had chosen to attend an HBCU. We were one step ahead of the game. The professors were preaching Diversity in corporate America well before it became a buzz word or "the thing to do".

My professors wanted me to graduate, but the degree would not come easy. I had to earn it and know that it would pay off in the long-term. My Career Center Director knew my name and would call me if I missed our weekly appointment. She taught me interviewing prep techniques, resume writing, how to research a company for job opportunities and a host of other marketable skills. I left my HBCU with PRIDE!

Why am I writing this Guide? I felt compelled to write this story not so much to tell the stories about Earl Graves, Morgan State University graduate, CEO of Black Enterprise,

Jessie Jackson, Civil Rights Activist, graduate of North Carolina A&T, Representative Jim Clyburn, Majority Whip 2007-current, United States Government, South Carolina State University graduate, Dwayne Benjamin graduate of Wilberforce University and Senior Manager, Novartis Pharmaceuticals, James Tolliver, Alabama State graduate, General Manager, Coors Brewing Company, Hank Allen, South Carolina State University graduate and Regional Manager, Pfizer Pharmaceuticals, Tchernava Rocker, graduate of Alabama A&M, Director Human Resources Harley-Davidson Inc. and a host of other billionaires, millionaires, and multi-six digit salary HBCU graduates I wrote this story to encourage and support the future graduates who will venture into corporate America.

Welcome, future business school graduates. The business world is waiting. You have some big shoes to fill. Are you ready?

Isiah's Success Tips

1. Identify and conduct a personal profile of yourself

2. The Career Center will enhance your skills

3. Be knowledgeable of the STAR Format: Behavioral Based Interview Questions

4. Apply for an internship in your field

5. Take a second language

6. Proper grooming is a must.

7. Study the book of a sport other than Basketball & Football

8. Get involved in your community

9. Learn how to market yourself

10. Master the skill of WorkingNet

Table of Contents

"There are 7 wonders of the world, you should be the 8th because…" *Reese*

Chapter 1

There are 7 recorded wonders of the world as told by the history books. However, the 8th wonder of the world is right inside of you. As I speak to students I often tell them that before you can successfully sell yourself to a company you must know yourself inside and out. Many of you believe that this is a very easy task right? However, it is much more difficult than you might believe. Yes, you know the basics, where you grew up, family surroundings, what you think you want to be in life, etc… Notice I said what you think you want to be in life. Dave Thomas, founder of Wendy's the hamburger chain once said, "Your first job out of college will not be your last. Find out what you want out of life and who you are." A point well made by a man that became one of the wealthiest men in the world by building a concept from the use of his daughters name Wendy.

It is extremely important that you interview yourself prior to going on an interview in corporate America. I have a technique that we will discuss later in this chapter called "Score carding ME". It is a process that will take you through the steps of how to view yourself. It will teach you how to set Objectives, Goals, Strategies and Plans (OGSP). As a future business leader in corporate America your challenges will be great. If you understand what your personal key components are, they will drive your success in the corporate world.

The key to understanding yourself is to first break down every little detail about you. For example, if you are strong in finance and lack interpersonal skills, this can be identified as a developmental area for you. During my tenure at my university, I realized that each of my business classes were building blocks to better help me understand myself. For example, during my freshman year, my workload consisted of foundational classes preparing me for what was ahead. During my sophomore year, the workload presented was more challenging and allowed me to apply some of the skills I obtained in the previous year. Junior year I took a large number of core courses. My Statistics class was a major challenge. I went into the course with an attitude of defeat. I was not a strong math student in high school and listening to other students that had previously taken the class, caused me to have a defeatist attitude. I had beaten myself.

Soon after getting in the class, I realized that I had created my own inner monster. You see the person that I was in high school no longer existed. Over the course of my first two years in college, I worked on my forward thinking. I found this to be very instrumental in helping me achieve a high grade in Statistics. What was the difference you ask? I utilized the "building blocks." The previous two years taught me how to identify and address areas of improvement. Doing so allowed me to round out my skill set and be a better performer long-term in the class room. As a senior, I was preparing to enter the "real world". During my last year, I stacked all of the building blocks together and utilized all of the skills I obtained and prepared to implement them in corporate America.

I am amazed when I hear students discuss their course schedules. "I have three core hard courses, so I need a non-challenging course". Does this sound familiar? Never once, did those students think about the fact that because they were interviewing for an internship that summer that the course they were avoiding would be key in helping them during that interview. This may be hard to believe, but I did not run away from those challenging courses or push them off because another professor was more lenient. The challenge to have a professor that was known for his strict rules and attention to detail was just what the "Doctor" ordered.

There are some very important lessons that I gained from my most challenging college instructors. They are:

- All course work was to be turned in on time with no excuses. *Future application:* those same expectations will apply in corporate America.
- Assignments were expected to be done correctly the first time. *Future application:* the expectation for someone with a skill set right out of college was to have a sense of how to do the basics of the job and does it right the FIRST TIME!
- Take pride in your work. Turn in your best work. *Future application:* Taking pride in your work early will carry over in your career. There will be times when you will arrive to work early, stay late and even work weekends to get an assignment completed.

How do I apply all this learning? I use what I call, "My Scorecard Personal Process".

My Scorecard Personal Process addresses personal desires and goals. Those desires that are key drivers should be used as motivational factors and aid in making decisions that will affect your future. They can be personal, professional and financial goals which will ultimately lead to the "Right Career Choices". It is important to note that you should place a considerable amount of effort in completing how you identify those three key attributes to help you get to know yourself. How many should you have? As many as you like!

When completing your scorecard, I do suggest that you make it realistic and attainable. How many did I use for myself? I placed three to four on my scorecard. Why? I believe that less is better. Remember, that is only because I feel I know who I am. Being blunt and candid is the only way to approach this exercise. Finally, make sure the goals are S.M.A.R.T-Specific, Measurable, Attainable, Relevant, Time bound.

Sample Scorecard for Isiah Reese

Professional:

- Become an official speaker with NSA (National Speakers Association) and Toastmasters

- Managing a Region within my current corporate organization by 2008 with a fiscal responsibility of $500-$800 million and managing a team of 50 plus people
- Become a Senior Vice President by age 47 with a fortune 100 company

Personal:

- Speak at my former university by the end of the year
- Send my parents on an all expense paid vacation by the end of the year
- Conduct the My Kid Biz conference www.mykidbiz.org and touch 500 kids with financial literacy

Financial:

- Purchase (5) additional Direct Stock Purchase categories by the end of the year
- Follow through on family being debt free with 18 months based on the strategic plan created
- Save $20,000 in an additional savings account

Seems difficult? It was for me! It took me about three months to narrow down from a list of ten in each category. Again, I prefer the less is better strategy. Do you now see how this can help you? As I stated, understanding who you are will help you knock down some of those corporate road blocks.

"My career center counselor was the best thing that ever happened to my life." *Reese*

Chapter 2

Isiah's Career Commandments:

1. Thou shall establish a record and a relationship at the University Career Center the first semester of thy freshman year
2. Thou shall meet with thy counselor once a week each semester
3. Thou shall take a résumé writing class
4. Thou shall take an interviewing class
5. Thou shall conduct a video interview taping session
6. Thou shall learn how to dress properly and professionally
7. Thou shall take a proper dinner etiquette class
8. Thou shall attend career fairs and pre-set thy interviews

I stand by my statement at the beginning of this chapter. I believe that the career center is the most important building on campus. It is only second to your major in college.

I was very fortunate to have the best career center counselor at my HBCU. There were times when I thought my counselor was the toughest person in world and often asked myself, why is she being so tough on me? I later realized that she was helping me develop tough skin for corporate America. For example, if I thought my résumé was good she felt it could be better. If I did not want to interview for a particular role, she would want to know why and have me to explain in complete detail my decision making process. It was a lot of work just to say no! It took me a few years to fully understand her expectations. (The DMP (Decision Making Process) will be explained in greater detail later in this chapter.) The commandments are the seeds of knowledge to help you build a successful corporate career. Once the seeds have been planted, it is up to you to make them flourish into a beautiful garden.

Commandment # 1: *Thou shall establish a record and a relationship at the University Career Center the first semester of thy freshman year.*

On your career path, there must be a beginning in order for there to be an ending. I have met a lot of crammers in my life and must admit to procrastinating on some projects over the years. I am the first to admit that I did not deliver quality work at the end when I operated out of the crammer mentality. I am here to tell you to get rid of that mind-set right now! Now, most of you are saying to yourself, I am a first year student why would I need this now? I have plenty of time! No you do not! Those eight semesters will be the fastest times in your life. I assure you. Notice, I said semesters and not years! The most successful people I know begin early and they separate themselves from those that think time is on their side.

The market for a career is not domestic, but global. You will be competing against students from all over the world. It is important to create a career center record even if you are in a field of demand, such as health care and education. This is only a win-win situation. Creating your record is the first step to the rest of your life. I have found from research over the years, that the students that I advised to do this were better prepared for the rest of the commandments and ultimately had much better success. Why? They understood the process and realized what it would take to get the job and career they wanted.

The career center has highly trained individuals that are there to help you craft your life and assist you in developing a path to get there. This is an invaluable service and would be quite costly on the open market. I advise you to utilize it now while it's free; otherwise you will pay in more ways that one later. Success is not free and neither are the professional services that assist you in obtaining that success.

Commandment #2: *Thou shall meet with thy counselor once a week each semester.*

I know this appears to be a very big order to fill, but it is very important. There is a cliché that says, "The early bird catches the worm." The career center counselor at your college/University can only help those that are taking their future seriously. If you think about the idle time that you spend sleeping in your dorm room or using your anytime minutes, those are valuable appointment times that you could have with your counselor.

The average amount of time spent with a career counselor is 30 minutes to an hour. Make the investment now. In corporate America you will hear the term, "learn how to manage your manager." Begin practicing this now. Your weekly meetings with your counselor will prepare you for those important recap meetings with your manager in corporate America.

They will help you to organize your thoughts and perfect the skill of verbalizing your thoughts to another individual. When you begin your journey in corporate America, this process will be very familiar to you and come very naturally.

Though the counselors are there to serve everyone, it is my belief that since I visited my counselor on a weekly basis, I was privy to information about upcoming interviews and career opportunities that others were not. There is a door that could open just for being in the right place at the right time. There are a number of people that walk through the career center and like any given Sunday there is any given day of the week that a potential employer could be there.

Finally, the budding relationship that will occur between you and your counselor will be immeasurable for life. There will be encouragement and direction that will carry forward in your life for many years to come. You are paying for this service as mentioned earlier in the book, so why not use it. This is about a commitment, so do not follow the path that many have chosen, and that is waiting until your junior or senior year to show up in the career center and expect something magical to happen. I am a firm believer that magic only happens in animated films, not in real life.

Commandment#3: *Thou shall take a résumé writing class.*

Well let me first say this is not your English 101 class. If you do everything right with all of the other commandments and do not do this correctly, then you have failed at this process. I know you are thinking, "This guy must be off his rocker." If I am, I have not been certified as someone that needs professional help. Follow me here.

The objective of the résumé is to set you apart from the competition and represent you well, the KSA's (Knowledge, Skills, and Abilities) obtained from your college or University. This is the most important document other than your social security card and credit report to tell the interviewer or company who you are.

The benefit to taking this class is most obvious. First, you will not get it right the first time; remember my counselor who made me do it over and over. Second, by understanding how to utilize strong verbs to highlight your accomplishments during your collegiate career allows you to better depict your accomplishments. Third, practicing this skill set while you are in college will help you once you enter corporate America. For example, as you start your career and you are asked to write a self evaluation, utilization of strong verbs will not only continue to make you stand out from your peers, but could result in a higher merit rating. Becoming a solid résumé writer will save you money in the long-run. Obtaining these skills now and continuing to build on them will prevent you from soliciting the help of a costly résumé writer. Who is better suited to express the role and responsibilities than the person that actually performed the tasks from the job? Once you become comfortable with how to construct a résumé, you will always update your information to keep it current. It will become second nature to keep your information current, even when you are not looking for another career opportunity.

Do not make the mistake as so many others have. Update their résumé when they about to look for another career opportunity. These are the individuals that have not reviewed or placed any new information on their résumé since they have been in their current role. Don't be one of these people. You should always be current with new concepts and ideas in your market and stay two steps ahead. Will you be ready when opportunity knocks? He doesn't always call before he comes.

Finally, the résumé writing class will teach you how to think through each and every detail about your career. After you graduate and begin your career quest you will have the opportunity to open several doors. Your solid education and preparation from your HBCU has given you a key that will unlock the door of your choice. One of the skills that allowed you to obtain this key is having a properly written résumé. Remember this statement, there are no ERRORS ever allowed on a résumé!

Commandment # 4: *Thou shall take an interview class.*

Some of you believe that because you had a job in high school you understand what it will take to land a major career in corporate America; think again. That is not a smite on those great billion dollar organizations that gave you your first job, the game is much different. In corporate America, you are not fighting for an hourly paying job, but you are starting your career with a job that pays you a SALARY!

During your collegiate years, you are a novice in the game of interviewing (we all were at some point in our lives and some are still struggling with it) and this is the arena to improve those skills. I made a commitment to myself during my collegiate career to learn to be the very best at interviewing. This is a very big challenge, but being the best is all I know and you should not be any different.

The importance of this class you ask. I am glad you wanted to know! The first thing you learn is how to properly prepare for an interview. Next the class will teach you about your tendencies that you have never noticed about yourself. For example, a tendency to say "uh" or to speak with your eyes closed. The class will teach you how to conduct yourself properly in an interview. It should go without saying, but NEVER EVER take your cell phone in an interview; it is not even acceptable to have it on silent or vibrate. Taking your cell phone in an interview is as bad as taking your cell phone in to church. It's simply not acceptable.

The importance of pronunciation and annunciation will determine if you are passed on to another face-face interview. Lastly, everyone needs coaching techniques so this is a mandatory class, not an option. Remember the old cliché' "Practice makes perfect"? Well, the more you practice answering questions in front of another person, or the mirror, the better you will get at perfecting this skill. No matter what industry in which you are seeking to get a position, your résumé will do most of the door opening. The skills gained from the interviewing class will make you ready and prepared when you walk through those doors.

Commandement#5: *Thou shall conduct a video interview taping session.*

I remember distinctly as if it were yesterday, my first interview session at the career center. I wasn't nervous since I've always been comfortable in front of a camera. Of course, this is not the norm for most people. I will be the first to admit that I was very disappointed by my performance. I was disappointed not only with my answers, but by some of my tendencies that were clearly displayed. This was hard for me to accept, because I have a very tough time accepting failure when it comes to performing.

The career center is the place where you want to correct these imperfections. Start early, this is not an over night process. What were some of my noticeable mistakes? I counted the number of times I said the word of "Um," as I replied to each question? I used the word um 50 times! Using the word um is a pet peeve of mine. It disturbs me when I hear someone speaking and there is an over usage of the word "um". I also had the tendency to tilt my head to the left while giving a reply. I speak with my hands, as most people do, and I was a bit overzealous with my hand movements. Finally, the most shocking discovery of all was the level of my voice tone during the taping. My tone was too low. This can be interpreted as the interviewee lacking confidence. This not something you want to portray in an interview.

Now that it has clearly been pointed out why you should tape yourself being interviewed, it's time to do it! Let's get you past the stage fright and determine the next steps. The first thing you should do is to contact your career center counselor and set up a mock interview session via video tape. Secondly, prepare for the interview and research the company. Third, forget about the camera and concentrate on the interview.

Finally, be prepared to accept feedback and critique yourself with complete honesty. It is important that you watch it several times. This is important because you will notice something different every time. Who should give you feedback? The career counselor, your business professor, a roommate and a business professional preferably in the Human Resource field would all have valuable feedback. I assure you that understanding what others are seeing during the interview is better than not knowing. If they're seeing it during a mock interview, it's guaranteed that these same tendencies will be noticed in a live interview.

Commandment #6: *Thou shall learn how to dress properly and professionally.*

I can not stress the importance of proper attire for an interview. As a student, I came to school with a black and navy blue suit and one tie to match both. It was a pitiful sight, but it was all I could afford at that time. I remember having to borrow my roommate's tie just to mix it up a little. I was committed to ensuring that my success was not going to be held back by my inability to dress properly for an interview. So what did I do differently? First, I had to learn the ins-and-outs of proper interview attire. How did I do that? A fashion coach was way out of my budget so I did the next best thing! I used my WorkingNet skills to learn how to dress properly. I went to a major merchant chain in the local mall. I asked for the manager of the men's department and made a deal with him.

I told him that I was a business student, it was my goal to become a corporate executive and that I was seeking his help. We negotiated an agreement. If he would teach me how to dress for the corporate world, I would purchase all of my suits from his store for the next two semesters. Did it work? Of course it did! He was ecstatic to schedule time with me for one hour a week for an entire school year. I had the opportunity to try on suits to determine what worked for me. I would watch the manager closely when he would sell suits to other corporate executives. How did this help? In the end, I realized that being taught how to tie a necktie in a Windsor knot, coordinating the right texture of socks with a suit, or even evaluating the fit of the suit wasn't the most valuable part of this lesion.

The one thing that stuck out in my mind the most was how I felt in the suit. The suit made me feel like a winner. It fit well and I looked great! As a result, my confidence was through the roof and this was carried over in my interview. I had purchased a winning suit!

Today, there are multiple resources to pull from. There are magazines, the internet, and of course, books like this to help you with your style. If you are not appropriately dressed, your appearance will destroy everything that your résumé and experience have accomplished. Remember, up to the minute you walk into the interviewer's office, it was your résumé that got you there. Now is not the time to risk it all with inappropriate attire.

Standard fashion tips:

- Men: A black, dark grey or navy blue suit with a basic white dress shirt is still the most appropriate attire for an interview. <u>The shirt</u> should be freshly pressed and should have a straight, tab or button down collar. <u>The necktie</u> should say POWER not style of the week. The fabric should be silk (if this is in your budget), it should coordinate with the suit, not match it, and should also reflect the tone of the organization and that of the person wearing it. DO NOT wear ties with symbols or characters on them!
- Here are a few basic color scheme suggestions:
  - Black suit: predominant color of the necktie should be red, burgundy, yellow or gold
  - Blue Suit: predominant color of the necktie should be the same as listed above
  - Always wear a pair of basic black socks

I suggest black shoes that you string up. Stay away from buckle shoes and loafers during interviews they are much too casual. The shoes must be in impeccable shape, clean and sparkling with a military shine. How you dress is a representation of you, how you care for yourself and by extension how you will care about the organization in which you are seeking apposition. . I personally keep two pairs of shoes that I only wear on interviews.

The accessories are easy. A nice watch with a small frame cut, not the trendy fashion one that is as big as my hand. Never, I repeat never, walk into an interview with an earring in your ear or any other place noticeable on your body. Lastly, keep the ring on your finger to a minimum as to not draw attention. If you are married, your wedding ring is fine. If single, wearing a ring is not necessary. I love my football championship ring, but sell "you" as a champion first. Your hair should be clean, neatly cut and well groomed. Facial hair should be neatly groomed or cleanly shaven. If you do wear cologne it should at a maximum be very light. Do not use abrasive or heavy fragrances.

- Women: A power suit: slacks/skirt and jacket; black, dark grey or navy blue. The blouse should compliment and fit neatly under the suit and not be too revealing, high around the neck or have too many ruffles or frills. White or off-white and soft pastel colors are acceptable. Pants and skirts should fit properly and not too tight. Skirts should come down right at your knees or slightly just above it, but no more than that. Keep the focus on you, not your body. Hosiery is a must and should be natural, sheer black or navy; which ever one coordinates with the suit. It is always a good idea to bring an extra pair, just in case you get a run. Never wear colorful or patterned hosiery, as this can be distracting. Shoes should match the suit and they should be clean and in top condition. High heels are optional, but if worn the heel should be 1-1½ inches high. Opened toe shoes should not be worn.

What about my accessories? A nice small set of ear rings should be worn. Large dangly and bulky earrings should not be worn. The watch should be small and classy to illustrate your style. If you are married, a wedding ring is acceptable. If you are not married, a ring is not necessary, but one ring is acceptable.

It is important that your hair appears neatly groomed and conservative in style. This is not the time to have the current hair trends. It is NEVER acceptable to have colorful and spiked hair. Perfume is optional. If worn, it should be very light and at a minimum. Avoid very abrasive fragrances.

From School of Business to Corporate America

Tips for men and women:

Fresh breath is a must! Keep a mini container of breath spray in your small carrying bag and slip a mist of spray in before the interview. Make it quick and unnoticeable. Finger-nails should be trimmed and hands clean. Ladies should not go overboard with bright, flashy nail polish colors. Eye make-up and lipstick should be used moderately. If you think these things are too picky, remember that it is often the small things that can eliminate you from consideration for a second inter-view.

It is important to note that styles have changed and will continue to do so, but, I assure you the key components of how to dress properly for an interview will always win. Do not underestimate the fashion conscientious interviewer. I have seen candidates that have lost their dream opportunity because they felt they wanted to change the system. Keep in mind that the person interviewing you is representing his company first and they are looking for the right fit in all aspects. So take the high road!

Lastly, have several copies of your résumé available in a leather portfolio. Inside your portfolio, there should be a note pad with your questions for the interviewer already written down. This note pad can also be used to take notes during the interview. Once the interview is over, ask the interviewers for one of their business cards. If you are interviewing with multiple individuals, make sure that you obtain a card from each person. Send each person a thank you note once the interview is over within twenty-four hours.

Commandment # 7: *Thou shall take a proper dinner etiquette class.*

Table manners play a key role in making a good impression. I will put myself on the chopping blocks for this one. I was fortunate enough to have a mother who was involved in a political party. My mother would host dinners at our home for the State Senator. My younger sibling and I participated in these dinners and therefore got exposed to how to behave at a formal dining event.

I grew up thinking a fork was a fork and a spoon, well, was a spoon. However, contrary to my personal opinion, that was not the case. My sister and I had to know what each utensil was supposed to be used for. We learned early on during the dinners how to pause for a conversation while eating and when to enter the conversation. Did we get a head start? Well during those times, I felt some of those events were quite boring, but as I look back there was knowledge being past from one generation to another. Knowledge that I thought I would never find useful; proper dinner etiquette.

By now the questions you may be asking are; where do I start? How much will this cost? Can I learn this from the internet instead? These are all good questions. Let's address the questions concerning how you begin this process.

The resources are right there in your backyard on campus. First, ask your career center counselor to conduct a table etiquette class. This should consist of the table settings, stemware, silverware and the use of the napkin.

Your next resource is the most obvious one. That place, where you go and hang out with your friends and get great food. Yes! I am talking about the dining hall on campus. Everyone at my University knew Mr. J, the Director of Food Services, but I think very few people viewed him as a resource for teaching dining etiquette. Mr. J would have been the perfect teacher for dining etiquette. He was responsible for setting up all of the presidential and major dinner functions on campus.

Dining etiquette is a learned skilled, do not underestimate it. Think about, who conducts the most dinners on campus? I know it was right under your nose and you did not realize it. None of us did! The second question regarding cost? It will cost nothing, but time, when you think about it. The internet can tell you how to set it up, but it can not take the place of actually setting the table yourself.

Dining Etiquette during an interview:

1. Allow the interviewer to sit down first; unless instructed otherwise by the interviewer
2. Gentleman, always pull the chair out if you are attending a luncheon or dinner with a female interviewer.
3. Upon sitting, when the waiter arrives ask him/her the location of the rest room. (Yes, go and wash your hands) You can regroup with your thoughts for those two minutes
4. This is a lunch/dinner interview, not your last supper, so order accordingly.
5. Do not season your food so quickly. This will tell the interviewer that you are quick to make judgments, before diagnosing the problem. (Not the kind of person, I want to manage my budget)
6. If it is a table seating four and you are left handed, sit to the left of the interviewer. As expected sit to the right if you eat right handed. This allows you to be in a commanding natural position to answer questions.
7. Order foods that are easy to manage; a sandwich for example. Make sure you slice the sandwich in two parts.

8. Never order alcohol during the interview meal! (Believe me it has happen to people I know) If the interviewer is ordering alcohol, you politely decline.
9. Ask probing questions; questions that require more than a yes or no answer. This is an opportunity to get to know the interviewer as well as allow them to get to know the professional you.

10. Finally, have fun!

How do I conduct myself at the dinner table?

- The indicator that dinner has started is when the host unfolds her napkin. This signals you to do the same. Place the napkin on your lap. If the napkin is a small luncheon napkin, open it completely on your lap. If the napkin is a large dinner napkin, fold it in half and place it lengthwise on your lap. The napkin should remain on your lap throughout the entire meal and should be used to blot your mouth when needed. If you are excusing yourself to go to the restroom, the napkin should be placed in your chair. If you have finished your meal, the napkin should remain in your lap until the hostess has finished her meal and has placed her napkin to the right of her diner plate. At this time, you can follow suit. It is not necessary to refold your napkin, just place it neatly to the right of your dinner plate.
- Foods you can eat by hand: bread, bacon, finger meals, foods meant to be eaten by hand, such as, corn on the cob or chicken wings.

- To remove an inedible item from your mouth, call as little attention to yourself as possible. Do so by placing your napkin in front of your mouth as you extract the item. To remove food from your mouth that you don't particularly care for, surreptitiously spit it into your napkin and keep it out of sight.
- Choosing the correct silverware during dinner can be an intimidating task. Let's make this as simple as possible. One should always start with the utensils closest to the plate. For example, the "small fork (J)", is the salad fork and will be the closest fork to your plate. The salad is the first thing you eat, so this is the first fork that you use. Please see the picture.

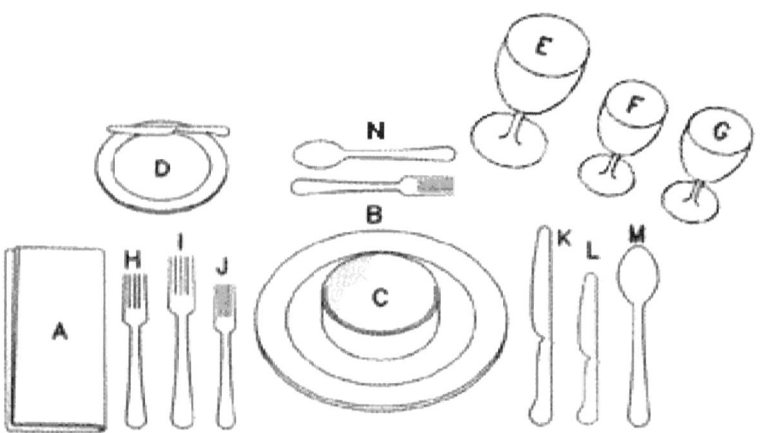

A: Napkin (placed in lap)

B: Service plate (dinner served here)

C: Soup bowl   (optional)

D: Bread/Butter plate with butter knife

E: Water Glass

F: White wine glass (optional)

G: Red wine glass (optional)

H: Fish fork (optional)

I: Dinner fork (used for the main course)

J: Salad fork (used for the salad)

K: Service knife (used for the main course)

L: Fish knife (optional)

M: Soup spoon (optional)

N: dessert spoon and cake fork

Commandment #8: *Thou shall attend career fairs and pre-set your interviews*

Isiah Reese

I know some of you believe that you can show up at a career fair your senior year and instantly receive a job. Well, contrary to popular belief, it does not happen that way. This event, organized by your career center, is meant to expose you to the different companies that are available within your job market. Please keep in mind, this is a screening process. Do not go there with false expectations, such as you are about to shake up the world... However, you should go there with purpose and the purpose is to get past the gatekeeper at the booth and land a live face-to-face interview.

The career fair should be viewed as an opportunity. If you do not take advantage of it before it is over, you closed a page of a book in your life that you can not get back. I have found that those who are the most successful at career fairs are those that have set up pre-established interviews with companies that will be attending. How did that happen? Remember that career center counselor? Is this starting to make sense now? I thought so!

Finally, come prepared with plenty of copies of cover letters and your résumé. This is your time to shine!

Be Knowledgeable of the S.T.A.R.

Format Behavioral Based Interviewing

Situational Task Action Result

"The STAR format changed the entire interview process as we once knew it." Reese

Chapter 3

During the 80's there was a sitcom on television entitled "Different Strokes," which stared the famous child star actor Gary Coleman. When Arnold (Coleman's on screen name) did not understand something he would look at his older sibling, Willis, and make the statement with this dumbfounded look, "What you talking about Willis?" It was hilarious to say the least. Well fast forward a decade later and though the sitcom is no longer there, Arnold's question is more relevant, but in a new format and it is now called S.T.A.R. Situational Task Action Result.

About twenty five years ago Behavioral Based Interviewing was created by the Behavioral Technique Group. They developed this format with the belief that past performance behavior predicts future on-job performance. There is direct focus on job related experiences, behaviors, knowledge, skills and abilities. These experiences can be professional, volunteer, hobbies, or even school related projects.

This technique is the most commonly used technique by Fortune 500 companies today. The days of so, tell me what you want to be in five years, are as extinct as VHS tapes. Welcome to the world of Blu-Ray Disc and it is called the S.T.A.R. format. I know you have a ton of questions. For example, "Is this a one-on-one interview or a panel interview? How may examples should I have ready? Yes, Yes, and my rule is to have three examples for a number of situational questions. So let's get down to business.

I know you are wondering what the interviewers are looking for from these behavioral based examples. Over the years, I have found that the interviewer is trying to determine three key things:

-Skills of Content

-Functional or Transferable Skill Sets

-Self-Management or adaptation skills

The content skill is knowledge that is work specific. For example, one's knowledge of being a computer programmer is specific to work that includes managing software and programming, not just using a computer. The Functional or Transferable based skill set is much more personal. This skill is around how well you organize and manage people, situations and your ability to communicate. The final one is very important for someone just entering corporate America. The interviewer is trying to determine if you are self absorbed or a team player. Are you punctual? Do you require a lot of self-direction or are you a self-managed person?

Yes, all of this can be determined from a series of questions and can determine weather you get that dream job. Do not think for one minute that you do not have examples for these behavioral based questions. You do! However, it is very important that you begin to build your examples. These examples can come from your summer internship, teamwork on a collegiate project, from an hourly job you have or may have had or from organizations where you have been an active member... Don't think of your examples as this grand adventure, they could be something as simple as an example showing how honest you are or an example showing your reliability. These are key attributes that the interviewer will be looking for.

Here are some tips on how to prepare for the S.T.A.R technique interview. First, as stated in chapter 1, it is very important that you "analyze your background." Determine how the three skills mentioned above are applicable and specific to the job opportunity for which you are interviewing. Secondly, you should be able to quantify your results whenever possible. For example, increased credential compliance from 70% to 93% in a 3 month period of time. These examples will highlight and illustrate your strategic analytical skills. Finally, keep a diary of your key achievements. I did this during my tenure at my University and it gave me the flexibility to choose from several examples when preparing my examples for interviews.

My company, Speak 2 Me Inc.^{TM} has specialized in the S.T.A.R. format for several years. We have trained over a hundred professionals and students across the country. These individuals were in professions such as Business,

Law, Medicine and Education. My best advice from this experience is: Practice, Practice, and Practice and develop those examples!

"By having some experience you will create long-term value" *Reese*

Chapter 4

Let's face it! The one hurdle that you will face as a new graduate is your lack of solid job experience. I know you are saying "wait, I just completed an internship, I have worked at the same retailer every summer, I have plenty of experience!" That is the one that I hear all the time from students.

I am the first to promote the importance of a paid or un-paid internship, and I am a huge advocate of the internship programs that are being offered at your Universities. However, they are not the saving grace and the instant key of your success.

Why should you participate in an internship program? We discussed in chapter three the skill sets (Content, Functional, and Adaptation) that an interviewer is looking for in a candidate. An internship allows you to hone these three skills and develop a broader range of knowledge, skills and abilities.

How do you qualify for an internship? Each school and university has certain criteria's that a student must meet to be considered as a viable candidate to be presented to a company. However, there are certain qualifications that I believe any student should adhere to. First, a strong academic record is a plus. Second, strong well written resume will help you set yourself apart from others. Third, a strong interview with key examples that not only illustrate your character, but your ability to hit the ground running with just basic guidance if given the internship.

For example, a marketing major interning with a major consumer products company brand team may get the opportunity to work on a project that is focused on a new marketing approach for a current brand. That person will gain the knowledge of Spectra demographic report, RACI analysis, trade marketing spend and return on investment when looking at a launch plan. The type of exposure from that opportunity would place you light years ahead of someone that has not been exposed to those things. It is very important that you work very closely with your career counselors and outside resources to find out who will be looking for candidates for that upcoming year.

Finally, the exposure to the corporate environment is of immeasurable value. Having the opportunity to view and meet other corporate managers enables you to see what is expected of you as an associate at that organization. More importantly, your work will be viewed by a variety of people within the organization allowing you to get accustomed to the feedback process essential to survival in corporate America.

Hello, how are you? Hola cómo es usted, こんにちはあなたがどうですか？, 喂你好吗？

Chapter 5

I have had the opportunity to travel abroad to other countries including Madrid, Spain in Europe, Mexico and Canada. While I enjoyed the social environment of these places, the knowledge and experience I picked up while traveling was has been of great value to me throughout my career. I had the opportunity to view different creative products and also learned how business practices were conducted in relation to those here in the United States. Finally, the long-term business relationships that I built have and will continue to aid me in my professional and personal development. These experiences have taught me to view the world from a wider and fuller perspective.

The evolution of changing demographics is continuing to matriculate at a rapid pace in America. Due to this rapid change in demographics, there are more restrictions being placed on illegal immigrants. There is a concern with this not only from politicians, but also in corporate America. The ever changing population has resulted in increased diversity in corporate America. The non-white population represents roughly 30% of the US population. Comparing today's non-white population to the population 10 years ago, you will find that the non-whites represented roughly 50% of the population.

What does all this mean for you? These are exciting times for the new graduate entering corporate America. I stated in my intro that HBCU's were preaching diversity long before it became the new buzz word in corporate America. The doors that were always being closed are now opening with greater ease. They are in fact, moving both ways, opening to allow you to enter the world of corporate America and sometimes closing so that you will have the opportunity to go forward to a better opportunity.

Does this mean corporate America has totally accepted minorities? Based on what I've seen during my career in corporate America, I can honestly say that there has been a wake up call. There is more Chief of Diversity Officers at Fortune 500 Companies than there were twenty years ago Think about some of the largest past and current law suits that some of these companies have and are facing. Let's face it, everyone wants to be viewed as "one of the great companies to work for".

Why the second language? It is quite simple when you think about it. One of my philosophy statements that I like to pass on is, "If you can not see the substance then it has no value in your life." What do I mean by that? Even though English is the dominant language in America and will remain so, you can bring much more value with upward mobility if you have mastered a second language. The opportunities I honestly feel are far greater because you have taken yourself from just being a domestic employee to a global employee. Another huge advantage that you will have is your ability to collaborate on cross-functional team projects that you may have otherwise been passed on. Think about how impressive it would be if you were selected to participate on a three month capability im-provement project for your company in Mexico or China. The message that I am trying to send, if you have not received it by now, is that traveling abroad during your college years gives you a global strategic vision on how business is conducted internationally. You will just set yourself apart from the rest of the crowd.

I am the first to tell you that the "Me too's" in corporate America stay right where they are. Those that exhibit zeal for knowledge and determination differ from their counterparts and will have a more successful track record. Imagine the CEO and the Executive Vice Presidents knowing your name because you generated a savings of several hundred million dollars due to your ability to speak a second language on a project. That is invaluable, professionally and personally.

It took me years to realize that I needed to learn to speak Spanish. Why? I looked at my current situation instead of my future. Will you survive if you do not take a second language? Yes, but being in the corporate world is about more than survival and a paycheck. It is about SUBSTANCE and VALUE and if you are not bringing either of those, you are a "me too". You may not like this statement, but here it goes. "We can find that person anywhere", we are looking for the very best. Do not walk off that campus without taking a second language and mastering it. I assure you that the long-term gain is well worth the effort.

"Do not leverage culture as a full house, when you only have a pair of two's." *Reese*

Chapter 6

Those that know me know that I am a huge Black history fanatic. I am a firm believer that your past will aid you in charting a path for your future. I will not spend the time going into the chronicles of Black history from slavery to the current. I will leave that up to you to study. Instead, let's talk about how using appearance as a means of claiming your culture will not help you in your quest to get into corporate   America. Let's face facts, to eliminate any misunderstandings. Point blank, the rules of the corporate world were developed by Caucasians. So in this case, I will defend the Anglo Saxon way of thinking on this subject. This is not about conforming. I prefer the term "conjoining". The conjoining method simply means that you will catch more bees with honey than not, don't you agree?

Despite the increasing number of diverse participants in the corporate sector the majority of those that still sit at the top in the corporate offices and in board rooms are white males.

The clean cut, well groomed appearance was established in a time when business suits were the norm and business casual attire was never even a thought as it is today. Although there are some differences today, the core aspect of the appearance is the same. I will put on my preaching hat like those old school ministers from the Deep South with the wooden buildings.

First of all, what you see on TV shows, the videos, and image confused pro athletes do not depict what corporate America is looking for. Some of us think if a star on a VH1 reality show can make it with a braided up look then so can I! Let's remember that this reality star was a rap star long before that show. He was a member of one of the greatest activist rap groups ever recorded. There is a lesson to learn from his success. Reinvent yourself once you are in the door; meaning, change your look after you land the job! Do not go in there with a look that will turn more people off. The look has to be appropriate and welcoming. What do you want the interviewer focused on during the interview? Do you want them focused on your "ethnic dew" or your credentials?

What people fail to realize is that it is not discrimination, it is assumination. Yes, I did create a word, but assumptions cause more harm than good. There is a big difference. Do not make the interviewer assume that you will fit in. Dressing the part is just as important as playing the part to get your career started. Often, I am asked, is this based on a particular college major. I will admit some of those whose careers are more artistic may get a pass at the graphic artist company. You however will not! There is nothing artistic about accounting and determining what will go in the credit and debit column!

The look is applicable to both genders! Granted, ladies may be able to get away with a nice professional braided up look during the interview, but if the hair is frizzled and the braids are old, this will take away from you during the interview. Guys, I could say that the women are worse off than you are, but that isn't true. Some of you are wearing your hair braided as well. Again, depending on the type of job you are interviewing for, braids "corn rolls" are not acceptable in corporate America on men. I have yet to see a corporate executive with braids.

I currently sport a bald head! We can thank Michael Jordan for that transformation! Yes, I drank the kool-aid and said, "I want to be like Mike." Here is the point I am trying to make, the professional image that you are trying to project should start at the top and work its way down to your feet. It should not start at your shoulders. During your interview, the interviewer will be focusing in on your face and what is coming out of your mouth. This should be visually pleasing to the eye as well as pleasing to the ear. Think about your future as you make the decision to change your look. I think Ludacris said it best after he won his Grammy award in 2007 for best Rap artist, "you mean all I had to do was take my braids out and cut my hair?"

As you can tell, the look goes across the board with entertainers such as Jay-Z, Luda, Busta Rhymes, 50 Cent, the list could go on. These guys got it! While Jay-Z was doing his American Express commercial and getting paid, you were struggling with the decision about hair or no hair! It is not a struggle, it is reality! In this case, take the path most chosen, not less selected. Take my word; there will be more people on that road, than the one you would have selected. I assure you the line will be much longer as you wait for that second interview, but at least your name was called for the first interview. It's up to you, which road will you travel, hair or no hair.

Study the sport of a book other than Basketball and Football

"To throw the deep touchdown pass in life you must first know the play" *Reese*

Chapter 7

Okay, I have to admit, having been a former football player at my beloved university, this was a hard chapter for me to write. I have played football, basketball, and baseball my entire life. They were my heart and soul. I thought I could not live without them. However, fast forward several years. I realized during my corporate career that those weren't the only sports I needed to be familiar with. There is one sport that I fell in love with and I still play to this day and that is chess!

Why chess? I actually learned to play chess in the seventh grade during an after school program. I wasn't really sure why I fell for the game at that time. Later in life, I figured it out! Chess has taught me how to play the game of life to a certain degree. As you study and begin to learn the game of chess you must first understand each single moveable piece. How they move, how powerful they are and how they can help you achieve what you want in life by strategically placing themselves in these small blocks which I call "life blocks."

First there is the pawn. Most people would view the pawn as small and not very powerful since they are the front-line soldiers with limited power to move. Contrary to popular belief, the pawns are very powerful in the game of the chess. They can wreak havoc by cornering someone, capture a valuable opponent's piece and once they have gotten across the board they can be replaced with a more powerful moveable piece. That piece will give you much more fluid motion of moving to win the game. How does the pawn apply to your potential move into corporate America? The one thing the pawn forces you to do is to think about your strategy, meaning, which one you will move first. Because the first move you make is the first step to determining how and what moves you will make after that.

Next, you have the Rook, which is shaped like a castle. This piece can move both horizontally and vertically across the life blocks. Actually, it is one of my favorite pieces on the board because it can cover a lot of ground with one single move. What is the relevance of the rook? Glad you asked!

Every time you take a class it is designed to teach you something about the core competencies that you will need to compete at the next level. By sliding the Rook across the blocks of life you are making strategic moves to make you a more complete person.

The next piece is the Knight. It is shaped like a horse head. The Knight has some special jumping powers. It can move both horizontally and vertically all at the same time, but within limits. The Knight offers up the opportunity to trap your opponent from an angle that you might need later. Yes here it comes! How does the Knight help me? Do you see a pattern here? I am glad you asked! Because of its ability to jump and move, the Knight suppresses the competition. By learning how to use this piece to your advantage, you can surpass your competition in the open job market. Think about it. In the earlier chapters I stated the importance of becoming totally integrated in the career center from your freshman year in college. You have just jumped ahead of your peers! You are making big moves, compared to their wait and see approach. This will help you even more once you get into corporate America. The game did not change; the moves will just be worth a lot more money.

The Bishop! In the game of chess this piece can only move at a 45 degree angle, but it can slide across the blocks of life from one end to another. A very powerful piece indeed! Help you how? The bishop is feared because of its power. The knowledge you pick up from each sliding block of life is important because you are being taught how to prepare for a business world that could chew you up, spit you out and leave you wandering around aimlessly for months at a time. When your roommate is asking why you are joining a fraternity or sorority tell them, "I am making a long-term power move". Why are you doing so much community service? A power move again! Why are you so anal retentive about getting your projects done so far in advanced? Yes, you are learning a behavior that will help you tomorrow in the blocks of life.

The Queen! Now they say, by every good man stands a good woman. This is the only piece that despite it being a "she", it is very gender neutral. The Queen is the most powerful piece on the board, make no mistake about it. This lovely lady has the run of the house as one would say. The Queen has no boundaries with her movement and can move in any direction at any angle. During your time in college there are a lot of moves to make before you graduate. The most important moves are those that you make with leaps and bounds that will put you into power like the Queen. Each time you think a "C" was better than you going after a "B" or an "A", you are not thinking or acting like the Queen. The behavior of the Queen is strategic, fact based and inquisitive. The Queen would want to know, why was achieving the higher grade so difficult. Did you blame it on the professor? Did you not understand the work? As you prepare to enter corporate America, the techniques that you perfect now, good or bad, will follow you into the business world. Each class has a meaning, even the most challenging subject matters. The relationships you build will help you if you nurture them while in school. Take the Queen approach, become the most powerful piece on the board by preparing for it and I assure you that it will be easier to move across the blocks of life.

Finally, the last piece on the board, the King! Now, from the outside eye people would have thought the King would have the ability to move across the board. Wrong! The King is trying to be protected because it is only allowed to move one block at a time. I believe the King is important because he sets the strategy for the others to make their moves. Though they are protecting him from being captured, each move through the block of life is one move that can help you move forward in your quest to transition to corporate America but without proper preparation you could make the wrong move and get captured in a web of self pity and blame. The King on the board would be you! So set the strategy and do not get captured.

Why did I take you through the game of chess? Did you think I was just going to tell you not to know basketball and football? Contrary to popular belief, a lot of company associates both male and female, participate in Fantasy football, baseball, and basketball teams. So, of course you should know those sports! Do I recommend you know the game of Golf? Of course I do! It is still true that a lot of deals and yes even promotions are discussed in those 18 holes. It is worth learning the rules of all the games. The competitive nature will come out of you and you will build some relationships that will help you make your "move" to the next block.

"Son, remember what the bible says "It is better to give than to receive". Acts 20 vs. 35 Mother *Reese*

Chapter 8

There are several key attributes that an interviewer looks for during the selection process and by surprise it is more than your résumé and good looks. The recruiter's main objective is to find the most qualified person for the company. That perfect fit includes finding someone that believes in the ethical values that the company stands for. If the company does not align with what you believe in, I assure you that will clearly show during the interview.

How important is community service? During your research about any company on their website notice the section that talks about social responsibility. We are in a time where there are numerous amount of financial and moral support needed for society. Knowing that, it is important that you begin to align yourself with some of these major organizations. It is important that the recruiter views you as not only someone that can help their bottom line, but also represent them in the public in a positive way. What are we looking for? That is a tough question, because there are some many great community service events out there. I hesitate to list them, because each has their place in our global economy today. It is important that you volunteer off campus as well as on campus. The advantage that off campus gives you is that you will increase your personal contacts for future employment and it will give you a different perspective on the processes to pull together a major community focused event.

There is no magical number of community affiliations you should be involved in. I will say however, that the quality of the events and your level of participation are more important than quantity. If you are given the opportunity to lead a special part of the event by all means jump in, but ask for help to assure that you do the very best job that you can do. I am such a big proponent of community service. I strongly believe it is vital for someone to realize that they can touch another person's life with just a little bit of time versus money. Take the time to get involved early in your collegiate career as it will pay dividends down the road.

Finally, I had the honor of giving a scholarship away to a high school student. Here were the words that were said to me, "One man's crumbs, is another's man bread." I will never forget that statement as it forever changed my life. I repeat it often to people when they question why they should participate in community service events.

"If a Super bowl commercial is worth $2 million every thirty seconds, then my career is worth $100 million and counting."
Reese

Chapter 9

Here are the famous words of my counselor at my University! "Isiah, just remember these words, "Sell, sell, sell yourself because you are the brand product." Funny how things resonate when you are caught up in the moment of interviewing, either on a phone or a face-to- face. The word sell is powerful enough, but her statement about me being the brand product is the one thing that still empowers me today. I do realize as much as I believed in myself on that campus, I needed some outside support to really make it happen for me to jump start my corporate career.

As a student, I believe you should begin to look at yourself as a brand new product just coming into the market. Like any new product you have to create brand awareness about yourself otherwise no one will purchase the product. That's how I began to look at myself while I was at my university. As marketing major, I was intrigued about how a product would be launched from inception to growth, maturity and then decline. I told myself that I wanted to remain in the growth phase and at some point in my corporate career transition into the maturity phase for a sustainable amount of time. The question I would ask myself, "How I was going to get that done without really know the ropes?

There is a distinct difference between a mentor and a sponsor. As a student I can see where you could intertwine the two because to tell you honestly, I did. I believe mentors play a vital role in your personal development as well as your professional growth. A mentor is the person who can provide a bird's eye view to things that you are seeing with a close-minded thought process. It is not because; you do not see the big picture. It will be because experience taught the mentor something that they could pass on to you. I have also found that a mentor will be much bolder with their advice to you; something that a sponsor traditionally will not do unless it is will help you with your professional career-pathing. It is important to note that a mentor will help you in the beginning phase of your branding process. A mentor for example, will drive home the point that you should keep your résumé up to date as well as your grades.

A sponsor is looking for the finished product in you. A mentor has a way of getting you to open up more about your personal life. A sponsor will listen, but keep in mind they are trying to see if those things will hinder you if they tap you for the next opportunity. Why do you need a sponsor in college? The path to enter corporate America is challenging enough and a sponsor is normally a person of influence at a particular corporate entity that can help smooth the path. He or she has the ear of human resource and other notable executives at the company. Building a formal relationship with this person is what I call the "extra key." If you practice and put all of the steps that I have discussed in this book along with getting some great guidance from a sponsor the road will become much easier.

Let me highlight a few points that you should look for in selecting a sponsor:

- Corporate Manager/Executive with a respected name at the company. (Yes! You should interview he/she)
- The person does not have to be a person of color. If they are not your chosen sponsor ask them to introduce you to

someone with your background to get another perspective.

- A person who is not afraid of giving you formal feedback.
- A person you feel very comfortable with.
- A person who will introduce and invite you to their circle of other notable corporate managers to help you land a job.
- A person who is willing to introduce you to the Human Resource manager at a company.

Finally, if you view yourself as the brand of choice you will win the job market over. The importance of selecting an influential sponsor can never be taken lightly. The road to a successful career has many turns and stop signs to get there, do everything in your power to market yourself.

"There is an art science to meeting people. It is called open your mouth." Reese

Chapter 10

I was once asked by someone that I had just met, "Isiah, have you ever met a stranger?" I had this inquisitive look on my face from the question asked. I responded with a jokingly answer and replied "When I think about it no." I have been born with a trait that my mother has blessed me with and that is the art of talking. My early experience with my father being in the Air Force and living in different parts of the country gave me and my younger sibling a leg up when it came to meeting people. Having been introduced to Asian, Hispanic, and German cultures allowed me the opportunity to see how those from other cultures conducted themselves in private and public settings.

The art of meeting people is a skill set that must be mastered, as you begin to make your transition to corporate America. Over the years I have taken the opportunity to practice and craft a technique that I call "Working Net." What is Working

Net? I have defined it as; *a collaborative session between two entities.* It is important that you treat each and every time you meet someone at a professional setting or in the grocery store as a potential partnership that will benefit you both.

Most would argue that this is the most important skill set to learn to get you into corporate America. The cliché should sound familiar to you, "It is not what you know, but who you know." In my opinion that statement remains important today. I understand knowledge, skills, and abilities should be the mainstay when it comes to your job search right? Those points are very important! Listen, I am not much of a hunting person, quite frankly I do not do it at all. But, I do recall my time fishing as a young man. I do not know anyone that has caught a fish in a dry pond do you? I like the statement, fish where the fish are. I am just constantly amazed that despite seeing some of these same techniques about the importance of meeting people students still take it likely. Just remember those eight semesters of undergrad and four semesters of business graduate school zooms by you like the wind.

I know everyone is not a social butterfly; otherwise there would not be such words as introvert and extrovert. I am an extreme extrovert, but as I mentioned from chapter one, I was able to identify that by understanding who I am. So here are some quick tips using Working Net.

- Join every professional organization related to business.
- Join the SHRM (Society Human Resource Management)
- Ask your business department to sponsor you to attend the local Chamber of Commerce business networking socials that are held monthly.
- The perfect Christmas gifts? Yearly subscriptions to Black Enterprise, Ebony, Forbes and Fortune magazines.
- Attend your school executive speakers series
- Ask your school to bring the BEEP program (Black Executive Exchange Program) to your business department.
- Ask your school career center to share with you any contact information for those individuals that they are aware of that in corporate America so you can contact them.
- Find out if your business school has an advisory board. If so find out when the next meeting will be held and meet those individuals.
- Go on your schools website and look at the schools Board of Directors members.
- Produce yourself some business cards with key contact information.
- Attend the National Associations of MBA conferences (Black and Hispanic)
- Local Rotary Club
- Local Chamber of Commerce

Once, you have taken the above steps, you must still "step up" to expand your opportunity for a successful entry into corporate America. So how should you step up?

- When I met someone using Working Net, I stayed in touch with them. This is important, because using a contact now is just as important as reaching that person later.
- Talk! Talk! Talk! Do not leave any stones unturned! Every moment is a career opportunity. Social affairs, sporting events that ride on the airplane, even at a wedding I have found great professional connections.
- Perfect key questions such as: Where are you from? What line of business are you in? What school did you attend?
- Engage in the conversation and listen, engage in the conversation and finally, engage in the conversation and listen to the speaker.
- Create a style approach. I am not abrasive, but I do like to start conversations. Understand your style and practice it so it becomes flexible based on the situation you are in.
- Finally, video tape you, in a mock play social setting with several people. This will allow you to notice social tendencies that you can improve on.

The Working Net is a wide spectrum. There are fraternity and sorority connections that will open a door to a great opportunity. I have personally experienced a career move with a Greek affiliation that catapulted a major change in my corporate status. Despite having a personal connection, it is extremely vital that you put your best foot forward during the interview process. The connection can get you to the door, but do not rely on your personal relationship as a Greek fraternity or sorority member to get you the job.

Finally, it is important that you cast your net of entrapment to catch your next opportunity. I strongly advise you to take every opportunity to introduce yourself to someone new at events because how they are dressed does not determine who they are. I may not dress the corporate attire at every event, but that is by choice. Do not judge a book by its cover as the saying goes.

Isiah Reese

Final Note

Today the United States is different from fifty years ago. There is an ever increasing amount of diverse candidates (along with the majority candidates) seeking positions in corporate America.

What I have attempted briefly in these few pages is outline how you can go from being ordinary to extraordinary in your search for a career in the corporate sector. Have I covered everything? No! But, I do believe that after reading this you will have a firm foundation on how to begin and what it takes to build that. It is this kind of information that will give you an advantage over those competing against you in this ever increasing competitive marketplace and its search for the very best talent.

www.ingramcontent.com/pod-product-compliance
Lightning Source LLC
Chambersburg PA
CBHW022128170526
45157CB00004B/1794